Adele
The Diva Chicken

Be Who You Are

 by Matt Reeves & Laurie Zaleski

Hi! I'm Adele the Diva Chicken!

I do NOT like laying eggs!! I like to shop and get my nails done!!! Where in the world does a chicken go that doesn't like to lay eggs?

We go to the coolest place ever, called the Funny Farm Rescue & Sanctuary, where over 550 rescued animals live!

Seriously? Who has time to sit around all day and lay eggs anyway when there is so much to do?

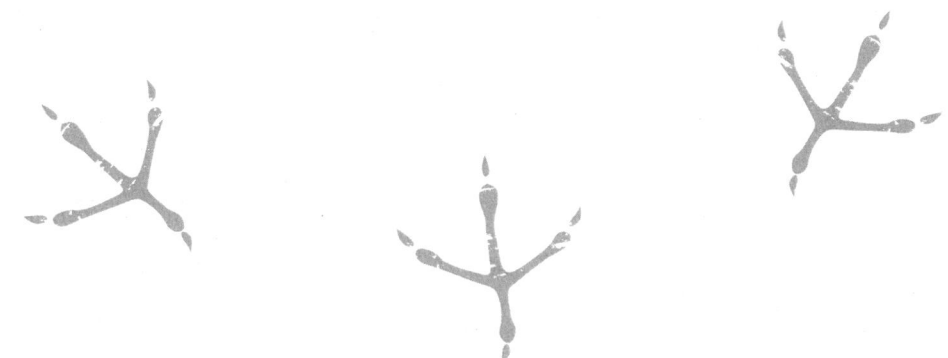

Once my sisters and I moved to the Funny Farm, it was SO nice! My sisters like to do something that I don't! They like to scratch around in the dirt. EEWW!

I do not Not NOT like DIRT!!!

Why do you think most chickens like to scratch?

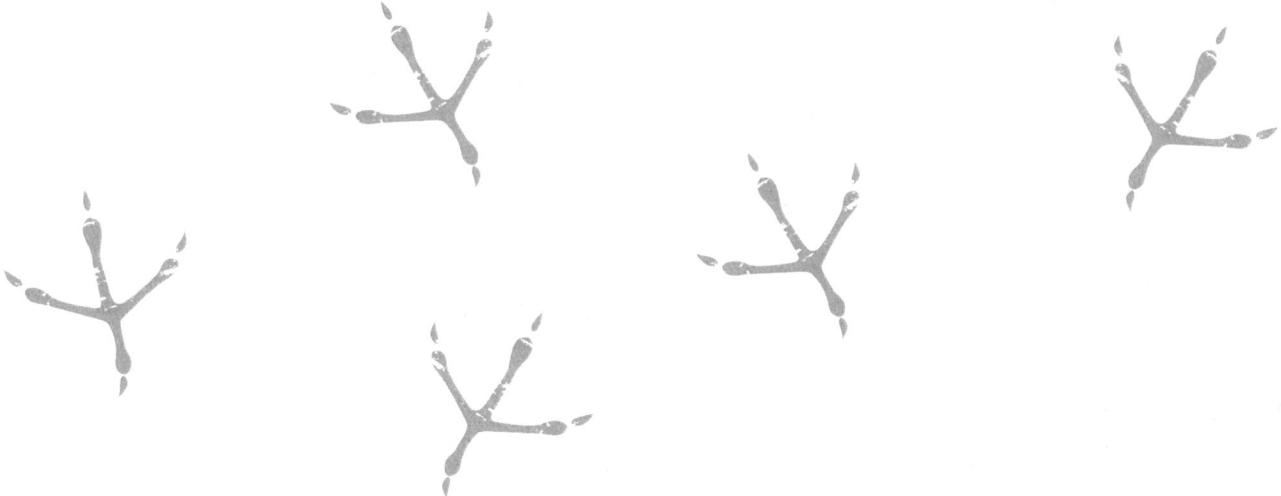

I don't want to live in a chicken coop. I want to live in the house and curl my feathers and wear beakstick!

I went up to the house and I kept saying, "Mom, Mom, Mom! May I come in?" - but only chicken noises would come out. So, I knocked on the door with my beak and finally, my mom let me in! It was the best day of my life!

Now, I live in the house! I sit on the couch, watch TV, and do what all girls love to do...daydream!!! Oh, and I wear a poopie diaper!

At first, I was mad and thought, who wants to wear a diaper? But then, I thought to myself that wearing a diaper meant I could live in the house and go anywhere I wanted to go! Now, I have diapers in all colors to match my nails and tutus! Diapers can be stylish, you know ..."Adele-Style!"

In the house, I dreamt of so many things that I wanted to be! I would sing and sing and never stop, so my mom named me "Adele" because I have a such a pretty voice and red hair!

In the house, I could see the horses running passed the window! I imagined I was a horse, because I think they are so big and beautiful!

Sometimes, they stop and smile at me and show their BIG teeth!

If I had big teeth, I would smile and show them off - all the time!

Did you know that horses have to go to the dentist just like you?

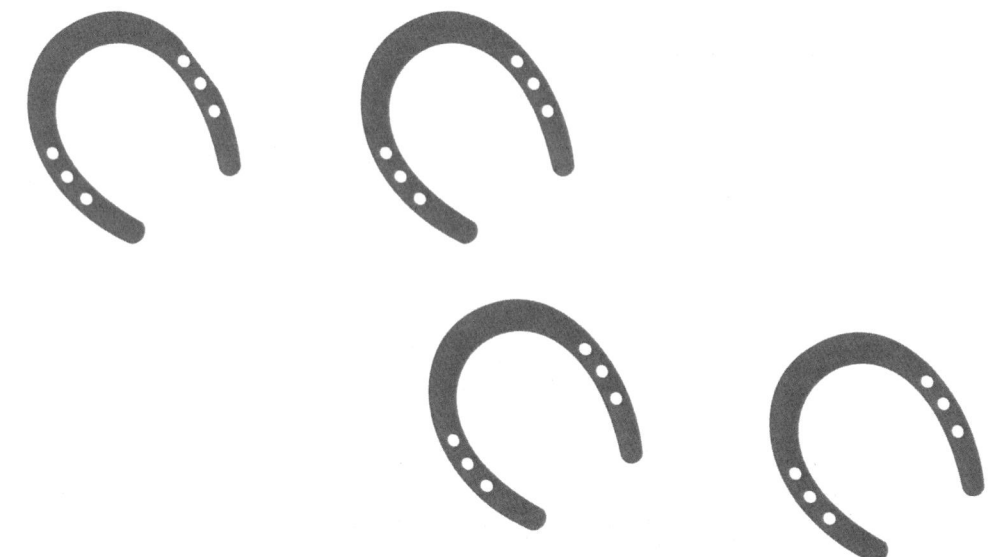

Ducks seem so happy. They always have something to say. They love to splash in the water and fly in the sky. Being a duck would be like being at a summer pool party every day!

I think being a duck would be fun!

I would like to be a goat because they are playful and like to climb on everything.

Goats have many unique qualities. They have four stomachs to help digest their food, and they have rectangular pupils which allow them to see all around them, even in the dark.

I think being able to see in the dark would be so cool... don't you?

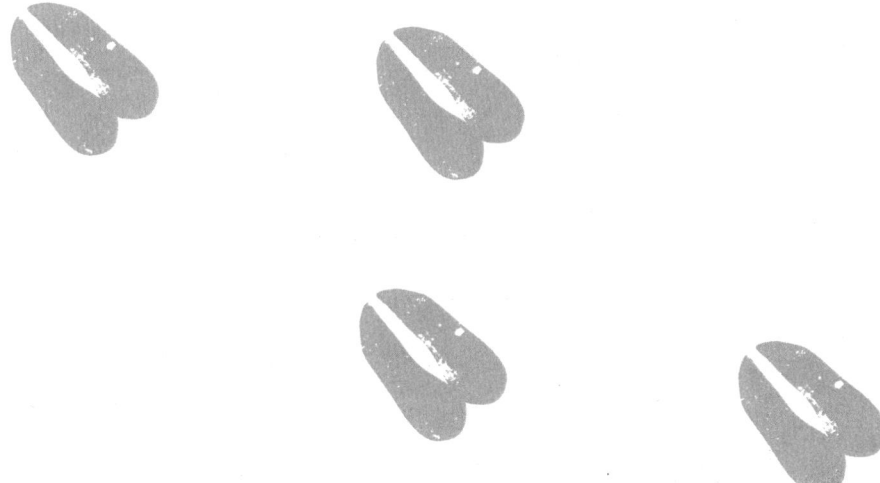

Kittens are soft, cute and cuddly. If I was a kitten, everyone would want to hold me and I would purr all day long.

I love kittens, but they sometimes play tricks on me and lock me out of the house!

Being locked outside is not, Not, NOT okay!!!

One of the prettiest animals on the farm is a peacock. They have so many long feathers and bright colors.

I would love to make my feathers stand up that tall and prance around like I was in a parade. Everyone would come from miles away to see me!

I have one brother who is very different from everyone else. He is mostly black with two white stripes down his back.

Do you know what kind of animal this is?

Sometimes, people are afraid of him, but he is very friendly. His name is Stinky. He stays up all night long and sleeps in the day.

I thought staying up all night would be fun, but I REALLY need my beauty rest!

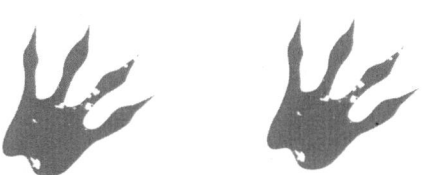

Lorenzo is such a loveable Llama. He has a long neck, long legs and very long eyelashes. He is almost six feet tall. I would love to be six feet tall!

Do you know how tall you are?

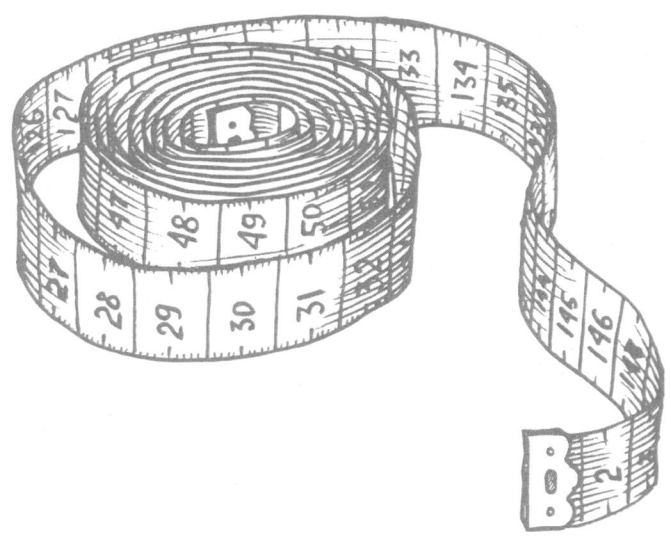

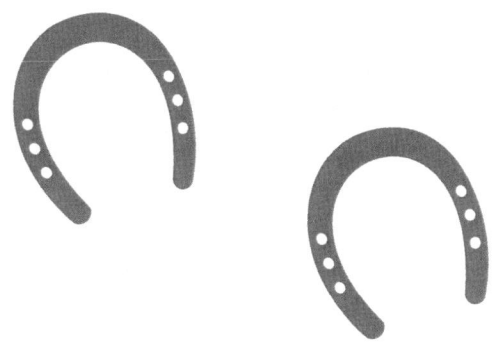

Sometimes, we all feel like we don't belong and that's okay. We look at others and think they have the perfect life, but you know what? They may be thinking the same thing about you!

We should always be nice to each other because you never know if someone is sad on the inside. Not being nice to others is not Not NOT okay!!!

It's so much fun to think about all the things you want to be, but the very best thing to be is YOU!

Always be proud of who you are because no one else is quite like you!

At the Funny Farm Rescue, there is NO bullying! Everyone just gets along. No matter what you look like or who you are, the best part is that everyone is different. That's what makes us all so special!

Be who you are and be the very best that you can be, just like me!

The End

-Adele, the Diva Chicken

The Funny Farm Rescue and Sanctuary is a real farm and home to over 550 amazing animals! Many were once hurt or had no home and nowhere to go. Now they have each other! Most of the animals roam free and happily play and go on adventures around the farm. Their lives and stories in this book are real. You can visit them free of admission on any Sunday or Tuesday 8 am - 4 pm at:

Funny Farm Rescue
6908 Railroad Blvd
Mays Landing, NJ 08330

Funny Farm Rescue is a 501(c)(3) charity and operates entirely on donations and receives no government funding. All of your donations go to the feeding and caring for the animals.

To donate:
www.funnyfarmrescue.org

To read more Funny Farm stories:

Facebook: "Funny Farm Rescue"